Little Hill

ALLI WARREN

City Lights Books | San Francisco

Cover image: "Pastoral," 35mm film by Joel Gregory
     © 2018 by Joel Gregory
Cover design: Linda Ronan
Typography and book design: Linda Ronan

Names: Warren, Alli, author.
Title: Little Hill / Alli Warren.
Description: San Francisco : City Lights Books, [2020]
Identifiers: LCCN 2019056680 | ISBN 9780872868052
     (trade paperback)
Subjects: LCGFT: Poetry.
Classification: LCC PS3623.A86438 L58 2020 |
     DDC 811/.6--dc23
LC record available at https://lccn.loc.gov/2019056680

City Lights Books are published at the City Lights Bookstore,
261 Columbus Avenue, San Francisco, CA 94133
www.citylights.com

CONTENTS

MOVEABLE C

It is in entering the street that I enter exchange

The loaded trees, the blooming thistle

The season of steal away in the middle of the muddle

Quartz in pocket, hibernating rust

My boss reads *Insights from Google That Will Transform How You Live and Lead*, my boss says all hands on deck

I don't want to apply verbal balm to accelerate the cogs, I don't want to put that mush in my mouth

Let the seas rise on the beachfront properties of the California coast and the glass in the reverse white flight lofts explode

You can't eat what you can't grow

Don't say milky white like that

What kind of fungus is this?

Slow burning night at home with my self-disgust &
    honey wine

Hovering above the heaving

There is no autonomous habit

The nub is smaller than the love in it

The equinox is not the solstice, I'm just trying to coax
    you to the damp upper limit

With my snout pressed against the tailpipe diagnosing
    time

With words as my coinage

Does "I will always love you" necessarily imply imminent
    abandonment?

To change things by changing their names?

To produce numbers and so produce norms?

I hear them singing "my love must be a kind of blind
    love"

If you're treading in the chop everything's a potential
    floatation device

Drug store talisman, pop-up dust bowl

Ghosts cheer from the dugout, spirits root in the shadows

I feel compelled to remain upright so I may be of some
    use rather than a reeking pit of pooled up resources

As soon as I start to speak, the crippling caving

Unintentional day of silence

Poached milkweed, lavender cupping

They say the way out is deeper in, but sometimes I wanna
    run

When the dead are laid in common earth, if there be light
    what the light might mean

What it designates versus what it legislates

"Embedded in things and not just in sex"

I study the past to denaturalize the present

Pink stucco shell, gooey rot center

Are mares really impregnated by wind?

There is a clock ticking deep inside the bedrock

The Door to Hell has been burning continuously since the
origin story

The threat is steely, latent, and inextricably linked to
everyday violence vigorously and unequally enforced

At the crosswalk an assortment of self-satisfied men hoard
clammy wads

A gloved hand extends from a tinted BMW to offer a
brown banana

The disorder is individualized

A cloud-based living package of commercialized affects
and capital functions

Radiating out across the land like so many orange
jumpsuits

You call it a god, I call it a menace

I've never been able to see the man who is his assumptive
face

The obstinate gait, the cocksure street

As if I get a warm feeling when he says good ol' boys
    state

He thinks we share a world, and my horror to the extent
    that we do

Where the cotton's fallow it's erector set suburbs and
    prisons

Bloated early boarders demand their champagne

I want to say the glass does not shatter it unfurls

Not here or there but in the mist

Our hero the velvet river, our hero the friend fetching
    another round

There is a possible future in a tender measure

An expanded geography of pleasure

The way out is across, in ardor

Let it burn bright in expansive night

I hear them singing "I hold out my hand and my heart
    will be in it"

Singing "the yam is the power that be"

The sun it sinks upon the valley, the sun it sinks upon the
  hill

The dead, electively present, conduit for all

The both/and meadow—beautiful and bleeding

Lover of the gray, don't rest in forgetting

Demand a future equal to polemic

Call this immolation love

The bones remember, gather around the legible bones

What will bring forth the toppling?

What kind of face do you want on your face?

The blue breeze at Connie's Cantina or the having-wept-
  into-your-omelette at Rudy's Can't Fail

Everyday I go to work

I mount my little saddle and pump the brakes

Riding through the gated residential, smiling at the stench

Have you received your perk yet?—flogged unconscious

The present is a tradition

Horror was not made in a day, that's history

What of its slippages?

What do bankers see when they leap from rooftops?

Blinding light of material day thrown across raked earth

"Every phase of capitalism produces its own ideal body"

J. Edgar Fuckface says "justice is merely incidental to law
and order"

Papas don't let your kids grow up to be strong silent types

The classroom, the workhouse, the patriarchal household

I prefer the whale's heft, buoyant in dark sea

To make of my breathing a fealty

"The difference between what we want and what we
want to want"

When will I stop being called young lady? I note it now
as a form of privilege & detriment

Anticipatory shipping, delivery by drone

Everything organized to deliver force on a routine basis

It's not that policy became any less racist, they just coded
the rhetoric and called it colorblind

They execute the writs to keep the blood, cum, and milk
out

"Orders are phrased as questions and compliance
interpreted as consent"

Who is permitted unhindered breath?

All I see is white lack, flowing through coffers

I want to make a leap that can't be turned from in the
rush of night I run from

I hear them singing "Oh no love! you're not alone"

Let's conspire in the sweat bath, let's do it beak to beak

Leave our pillows out to gather up the air among the
glade

My responsibility is to others first and from this I come to
myself

Can power entrenched unequally be withdrawn by sheer
    force of individual will?

No song alone can compel the maw to retreat

It's congealed in my romper and in my phone

The festival is full of missionaries, traders, and
    government agents

There are so many men in this place all fragrance ceases

Happy New Year, Total Loss

Billie bends a quarter note and everybody sighs

I hear them singing "life is too short to have sorrow"

Angela Davis wrote her autobiography at 28

I take my legs out to the edge of day and watch the
    commute make its slow way up the hill

One's dress, demeanor, movement through public space,
    tone of voice, companions

It's more expensive to go to work than to stay on the rolls

It's cheaper to be on probation than to pay for a monitor

I emerge ambulatory into the night with distended snout
and jowls

If in his eyes I think I see contempt, is that paranoia or
intuition?

The disorder? Global

Self-diagnosis? Nearsighted

The way into some better measure might be under water

An animal is accurate unto itself

My body clock rings in line with office time

I'm nostalgic for what I've not seen in the world

The rebellion was not spontaneous, or the consciousness
of its actors was not

If we underestimate it, we will not be any closer to
dismantling it

The function vs. the particular one who embodies this
function

"As long as men have rights in women which women do
not have in themselves"

With the ruby red wedge for breakfast and the frosted
flake pét-nat for lunch

I lay into the fragrant air and kiss your little windows lid
by lid

The wind rustles through elephant ear, kangaroo paw

I'm a fan of the amorous, I like the shapes of unwavering
love all lined up in its costumes

The scrubs and berries and bitter sidewalk weeds of
making do

I hope we can be buoyant together in the break, I hope
we can be forked

VISUAL LITTER

It was during this time that I was most asleep

Pecking at possibility in wastewater

Over greyhounds and manhattans

Over beers and ciders and spritzes and vermouths and
sherries

There are lots of ways to measure the same feeling

Some persons in hats are walking around on a roof

Some persons are beating skulls and shopping on bone
heaps

The dollar we exchange means our palms don't touch

The tearing, cutting, chewing, and balling up of food is
for digestion

Which is the transformation of milk into blood

Behaving like accounting

Constant as it flows

And it goes on behind our backs and in plain sight

A hoard that flexes in flux

Monetizing the waste of the problem

My person or rather my pocket

Alternating heat, cooling, and light

I cross traffic to sit at the fountain but the fountain is
gross

I err when I naturalize it

Will you understand my messages even though I don't
have a tail?

I pass mile after mile of excessively verdant fields

I tell the sun and the crops to get a room

I move to Prunedale to reconnect with nature

By which I mean prunes

It is there where I make my discovery

The kernel of the walnut is a brain

And the human brain is modeled on the walnut's success

On the scale of how I'd rank the elements

"To be alive, to transmute, to be melancholy under the
moon"

The seasons go: poppy, Penn Valley, particle mask, braised
meat

The court summons me to report to Martinez, home of
the martini, but I don't believe it, and I don't believe
the courts

You place your phone atop mine to transfer its charge—is
this the communism we deserve?

Where every eye is a beak

The landlords think themselves princes

And the cops, we know, are deadly

A many-headed wall of soot

I want to tongue the word ab-o-li-tion

I want to learn the lesson of worship from nature

No locks and no clocks is the way I want it

Up around the breasts and the berries and in the bath

Eternally recurrent reenacted enclosure

I plug up the mouth of my burrow

Subjection may be stressed on either the first or second
syllable though 72% of the usage panel prefers stress
on the second, stress in general

In order to live one must come up with the money

I cannot apply for the Head of People position at that pay
rate

I am not qualified to be a Cloud Engineer

The market will close and if the market closes there will
be no fruit eating

There will be no pit throwing

Or casting faxes across a sky in which the sun is setting

Or singing torch songs in a living room in which the roof
    is caving

Under wettest clouds

The bridges span the water and the river nets

The sky mall rims the perimeter

Lindsey establishes a psychic office

Rivka's driver Moses leads her out of Woods and into the
    arms of Alameda Island

I am trying to bury my mineral body in the earth and air

The flower is the force, light is concurrent

The hail fell on me but did not strike me

Brushing ash from windows, using the hair on my arm to
    do it

Among the fortifications

At the back of the bulb of the eye

You can use it as a door or you can use it as a door

"But to say it is hidden, remote and elusive is not to say it
does not exist"

I am learning to spell "unallocated" in wooden alphabet
blocks

I am waiting for the right time to touch the tunic of my
heart's desire

Devoted to the way light catches the folds of the hill

Flotsam is the foundation

Worms make culture in the dirt

We could not be convinced the land was not collective

We drink from it bathe in it and eat around it

Like an egg pollinated externally or the wind with its
flower

I found myself sleeping on one of its portions

Strolling around like a subject

Speaking about a who as though it were a what

Where the streets are paved with oranges

Just because I make one decision doesn't mean I won't
    ever have to make another

There is mountain on Mars 65,000 feet tall

That's a long way to go for some lichen

I'm grateful the market put an iron sheet over my face

Lay me in bed and bid my prosecutors hasta la vista

This is the cake that got rained on

SCRAMBLED EGGS

For the night, which is droning

"Under the moonlight, the serious moonlight"

The lawlessness of the ocean is a siren call

First comes the eye, then comes the weapon

A speed bump in the midst of apprehension

A cluster bomb of red projections travels up California's
spine

Is a sign a source?

Unemployment is built into the fabric of the wage
relation

Flyknit health core, green juice purgatory

Another apocalyptic water dream, momentary house of
unqualified desire, damp stillness of early morning

The lily at rest, receptive, the unity of its gyre

A shiny new traffic cone, a snow bright hole

I pay for the feral sour ale with my maladaptive grin

I stick my nose between the rusty links to get at the new
jasmine

The fragrance is boisterous, for entire blocks I stroll

Tongue folded back on itself like a reluctant taquito

I hand Sam eighty dollars, he says happy paradigm
hunting

Is this what they mean by livability?

Toast sandwich with a side of grass salad

Branding a holding pen a welcome center

The Asiatic Barred Zone, the Misery of Maquiladoras

First comes disgust, then comes marriage to morality

Retching into the mulberry, then adopting that position
as righteous

Keeping the corporate body in shape

Harpooning the raft of those in need

They offer an endless array of congealed shit, sometimes
on sale

The biopolitical arc of the universe trends toward Fitbit

Mandatory self-reporting is optional but strongly
encouraged

My irrational body wills illness, interrupts production

Is it possible to sort a spreadsheet while flat on your back?

Why is the playing field blue?

How does the iris find its object?

Plunder culture, culture plunder

He works hard to ensure his consumption is visible

My tactic (the opposite) is perhaps no better

Queen Eliza-fuckface draws a blood-red X over an entire
region

An endless catalog of extraction, of produced and
sustained misery

They're gold-mad, they even sweep the seams

My constant container, though it leaks and bleeds, has yet
to utterly burst

Please, an apparatus against perpetual shame &
hopelessness

A locatable shale gate, the field, its animal exuberance

A shovel-ready heart-shaped ass

Bare thighs on damp grass in the humidity of an
evacuated August night

Or true orange crush

"it is terrific / To learn something about the unknown /
By dint of sheer desire for it"

There is nothing remarkable without you to see it with

What I project as unattainable or impossible so there's
no need to venture into risk, so the dream's forever
cathectable

How I bemoan that Monday morning return, yet huddle
off to my caving station

Pointing at the rift, the coastal range, the cognitive hill

Displacing structure onto the individual

Instrumentalized as expendable, institutionalized as
  disposable

The landscape woven with displacement and purled with
  chokeholds

The winners win by others losing by force

Wraparound at the 20, bearhug at the 5

Assuming the content is static, the category knowable

As if sexuality were nothing but a catalog of holes

What would it mean for ears to find their own will?

Are feelings tactics? can emotional life be radicalized? can
  I sweep away their ideology? what will be left?

A bunch of neon yellow carnations in a blue plastic
  bucket molting in desert sun

"Underdevelopment isn't a state of development, but its
  consequence"

Chelsea boot with a Crossfit booty

The condo kills the neighborhood in two months flat

Your portfolio is reeking

But what is causation really?

Going into debt so as to be employable so as to slowly
or never pay off that debt or having been born into it
or to always already be considered unemployable or
disposable

The seepage is everywhere, you can never cut clean
through

First the invention of joblessness, then the landscape
envisioned as an endless succession of cellblocks

The border makes an unruly gate

A woman aboard a vessel is considered bad luck

But my right to white life is never officially questioned

"Those who choose the lesser evil forget very quickly that
they chose evil"

It's not a consistent type through time I want but
enunciation in acts

Cleanliness is secondary, the point is to drench myself in
scalding hot water

The listening chambers on either side of my head
  collaborate to produce a metronome

How can I preserve my body without preserving its
  exploitation into labor, how can I care best for yours?

The curve of your clavicle, the nook for my nose

The evacuated space where your living breathing
  extension once thrived

Where matter does not take form until it is observed and
  the agora was never not policed

A sea vessel may fly any flag but still a flag it must fly

I venture into the swap meet to buy back my car coat

It may look like conducting business but I'm mapping a
  route back from working dead

Hailing heavy gray oak hibernating like a teen in their
  bedroom

What does it mean to have "good boundaries"?

A pointer parts the lips and ventures slowly past the
  threshold

Baby's-breath white bright green spume

A Leo in the twilight of their mane

Fidelity to the cannon, flatulence in the common soup

Satellite wrist for the patient, data management for the
caretaker

The quake won't shake the landed from their palaces

The burst of heat from the tumbler lasts only as long as
the stairs extend to the street

What's that smell?

Autonomous ooze

Impenetrable, cordless meat

The finches host their lunchtime meetings in the fir

As long as the river's been running

First as contingent decision, then as official history

In place of an offer, an imperative backed by guns

The very sphere of work which makes it possible in the
first place

To solve the problem by exterminating the person

I bite my tongue and try to be a pleasant patient

Clinging to the vape for dear life

Out-of-home boost, work-ready blow

Wild mustard thriving atop what we can't be sure is a
butte

Or should I not again utter ardor?

What's the difference between vulnerability and
openness?

Trained to hoard but preferring to forage lightly in the
grape green field

Employing my time in such activities as daytime sleep

My end zone dance is planting bulbs

Should sensuality produce guilt?

What if instead of the idea of the future what we really
love is malleability of the past?

But you know how women are

I make a barrier of my aptitude, a conundrum of my
inclination

Somersault in the infield, cartwheel on the warning track,
    and the sod between

Thumping into the life hole

The constancy of its splitting

The whole earth under long barrel

I scoop the hardened yolk from its white crib

A holler is a hill one should run from

SEBASTOPOL

When I am in my fevers and frets I go to the trees

To sit befuddled at the base

Having never learned moderation

I want to keep the time that bougainvillea keeps

When nectar is scarce

To flit about the flowers

Like bees taught me

At that lap I sit and sing

Intentionally outnumbered

I learn that a fig is really an urn

The flowers of the fig tree cannot be seen

They are abundant, the urns

Lurking about hedge strife

While Duluth awaits its climate migrants

There's good food and drink to be had

While the catastrophe rolls in

We're stocking up on jars

They'll find us under

All the jars

How do you teach a dog to bark

You don't?

I say hi to myself

In the mirror

Or is that not a mirror?

The air is full and you are not here

I put my hand through the oak

I use my fingers

To make the object do what I want

I don't apologize because it is a machine

And I hate machines

I apologize to the bee

I find near-dead on the carpet

And to the leaf

I take down from its dancing string

But not to the machine

I follow the sunlight around the lawn

With a ridiculous green plastic chair

A chair has its task and performs it well

What is mine, listening?

I didn't make a sound until I was 2½

I have to work harder because I am dumb

With cause to wade into water

I'll take that shimmering

Over all the gold

Standards made by men

If obsolescence is inherent

Do I soak and savor

Or fear and plan

Knowing it will die

This feeling will die

The arbor is deafening

The wood is there to make hollow make sound

The gin is there

So you taste the pepper

I get dressed so I can roam

And sit under oak

But mostly I get dressed

To go to work

So I can eat and occasionally

Fill a tub with water and soak

The bankers do their different voices

Their hearts are blotted

Against those simply trying

To make their way

Against death

They breach morning light

That most intimate light

With surges of work

I feast on plastic

Plastic tastes good

I think that sound is a horse

Though I can't be sure

If I wear blue

The sea won't feel so vast

If I watch my step

And open the gate

And leave the yard

See how the animals

Move and the coloring

We try to be friends

Though I have no tail

I ask the horse

To come near

I ask the sun

And the poplar

After I learn its name

Tallest tree

Gets the most light

Thirstiest duck

Gets the gruel

I place my head

Into the grasses

And a bug falls dead

But it will come alive again

In the juice of my body

There is no color but the sun

And with my ears

There are spores

Hard thinking spores

The gray door

Is not my fault

The water tastes like

Not water

So I fill up on beer

Is that a miniature statue of a purple cat

Meditating in an Adirondack chair?

I am naive

In the ruthless world

Among the goats

I try to predict your mood and fail

Having moved through so many moons

I come out the other side

Returned to the center, love

Should I be embarrassed to say it?

In the evening it is bird time

And I miss you, all of it

I don't make it very far

In my short interpretation of travel

Without noticing you

Beside me there

Like the stars are

Plump, oblivious

If I wish for more

It is not because I mean to tempt them to punishment

If I wish for more

It is not because I am impenetrable to air

How big is that bird

On the barn bush?

How big is that bird

On the bay laurel bough

The trees have eyes

Where they've been lopped

I try to catch their gaze

I mean I weep and whiff

Into the dirt

Into the mincemeat

The thing I want most?

A different hill to die on

Thick and tall and radiant

In the mountain of air

When we kiss

Bark against my back

As if someone opened

The blinds and let the light

Stream in

There is gray green

And red green and golden

Light green and grass green

And lichen green and moss green

And the soot of the lemon tree

Which Erica says needs iron

Does loving this way

Prolong the war

Or the world

Or the people in it

At the base of Marin County

Sits a prison

At the seat of all counties

It is because of the little ice age

That we have the sound of violins

The ice age is music

Ringing asunder

In abundant air

With what is coming

Down the hatch

We'll have the sound

Of a new music

Of a different density

Ringing asunder

To humanless heaven

A wide tongue

Clacking a clear bell

Under the ocean

A sapling threads the gate

To get to where the light is

I accord it sympathy

That's my snout

In the feed bag

In late afternoon

I have come here

To sit on a box under a feed bag

And measure time

By the swarming of the worms

I've been outside the length of a working day

And seen hundreds of leaves fall

And what sound like seed pods

Though I can't be sure

A current of air gradually gains on my skin

I walk to the temple

And try to signal the horse

But it is sleeping

And I am awake

I take dictation from the leaves

The little brown ones

But my favorite is the amber

WATER AND POWER

Eating a freshly fried egg at 10am is one of the ways I
    indicate to myself I am experiencing a day without
    compelled paid labor

I've called in sick and it's warm, the sky's blue

People say the light is different in California but I've been
    here all my life

People say you can measure the size of raindrops by
    examining the colors in a rainbow but I've never tried

I carry my symptoms to the pole past the metropole,
    waist deep in marsh muck

The bell rings as the waters rise over the base, which is
    what generates the winds, with the flows and with the
    floods

The population is assembled and made to produce a
    surplus

Rations are parceled into beveled bowls

Shocks are absorbed by unnamed unfortunates

I push paper for students steering Teslas

They pump groundwater from boreholes

"The rich are only defeated when running for their lives"

This the building song, the current carves the course

The green open-office is constructed of congealed bones
and guts

The millennium tower is sinking

Every day I am covered in water twice and also uncovered
twice

The cat and I sit and listen to Phillip Glass and our ears
perk up

The cat is a loan, like the house and the Honda

Our transaction is fulfilled in symbolic form

We are strangers to each other

Sub-prime subjects shellacked into liquid lives

Sometimes I rebel against the slop and treat myself to a
salad

I throw my belongings out to sea and this brings me great
prestige

The ATM'll "shit money if you know what numbers to tell
it"

The land is scrubbed and repurposed

They build prisons on fallow fields because there had
been drought

Because there had been drought fires rush across the land

To fight fires they use the labor of the people they
imprison in cages

My brother says if people in cages accept pennies to fight
fires that's their choice, I ask my mom how he got this
way

My mom gave birth to me, child number three, when she
was 34, the age I am now, childless

What is the water doing before the ducks disturb it?

If we stay real quiet will the landlord forget we're here?

Clomping through the market, munching on the carrion

After the geese have come and gone

In the wake of the break

I rush home to curl into the last slice of light penetrating
the house

On that slice, on this abiding earth I stand

It wasn't the truth but I knew with certainty it was true
to me

They push poison pills and heat-seeking fangs

But our skin is supple and tenacious with fellow feeling

And we can slip like ghosts into the water

Past the dune, the foredune, the berm, the beach face, the
trough, and the bar

Knowing what we refuse

Our obscurity is due to being made of our surroundings

And if you move through that, repeatedly, you can move
through anything

I was taught my skills in the meeting house and also
   under the moon

In the material sphere beyond private skin

I was taught yews came before churches, property is
   plagued, keep your top eye open, make wine from
   plums

Remember to balk when the engineers speak glowingly
   of the human-like countenance of the delivery drone

The robot on Dwight and Shattuck collapses, I mean I
   collapse it, I kick it to shreds

My paycheck is a ration, my paycheck is a ration, ask
   forgiveness

Along the edges of the scrum, ask forgiveness

If penance is a pendant, how often shall I wear it?

Poking the administrative tablet, rasping at the door of
   HR, 18,000 hours and counting

The warming is faster than the models

A new border is thrown up everyday

I keep the reeking document in my pocket to prove it

In Vancouver they tell me if you caress a dollar you get a
whiff of maple syrup

First I put a bill in my mouth and munch and then I use
a nickel

In preparation for the procedure, it's best to evacuate the
guts and refrain from nostalgia

Squirt three dabs on the rag and try to disappear desire

But if I scrub off the evidence I'll have no heart left to do
the pumping

The sun is a clear, persistent, and beckoning door

The way a singer throws their voice against a rising and
makes you feel a thing, I feel a thing

Watching your chest rise and fall, the rest of the world
thrown sideways

My hunger overcomes my caution

In bouts general, random, and frequent

I didn't yet know the ground itself could rot

And my language consists chiefly of flags

And what would I really do in the woodwork anyway, I
    can't even find due north

They claim there is an unfeeling part of the horse

They say Shirley Jones died with her caretaker in the
    fire—they don't name the caretaker or the pre-existing
    condition, the endless and unequal toil

The cure is as ruthless as the illness

The fault lines are byproducts of the foundation

The goodies are on the bottom, arrayed like potatoes, in
    the ground, in the ground

I am harbored there, root by root, tutored by your love

When we were peers of the realm and looked up under
    the clock tower

When there was still a there, when we are alive and there
    is a breeze

I set the idea of it in my bag for safe-keeping

I go to the green and blue and construct a series of
    windows

Squawking cat bird, light behind the leaf, patty thriving
    underbrush

Abscond with the alluvium and forsake the pouch

Though it be light, though it be light

Float it down the water

Where I find my companions where I left them

Where I hide a small plot in the forest

Let the fleece of our fleets be fruitful, let we be warm of
    thought

Let the paper money men and goldbugs find their necks
    mud-raked

I want this like I want a long weekend, a kiss in a dark
    bar, a slug's trace across some lichen

There's lots of little birdies hopping around in the grass,
    the rich are running for their lives

They say it's an immaterial, promissory, and imaginary
    feeling, although not unreal

LITTLE HILL

Like any animal I need

Something in the morning

To rouse me

The joy of my friends

Against this Fidelity Investments notebook

A gift from my brother

I use for its hard back

To rouse me

To lose myself against image

Against the trading brokerage of choice

I need a patch I need a sticker

I need a sticker and a new world

No splendor untainted

Is this mourning naive? selfish?

To want the apple

To propagate itself

To want the syrup and the songs

I do not believe we know

What will come of any action

Considered or directed or righteous as it may be

Desire is not will

Fidelity to what?

There must be pleasure

Eating and shitting and fighting and fucking

With this marking and with this fire

The flood through which the blood runs

Knowing the thing by its disappearance

Wading in noxious waters

Bathing in the backwash of our cities

My phone beeps

I read the news

We used to throw trash into the ocean

We're more subtle now

I slip into my microfiber

I get ready for work

I've been taking heart

In how quickly the sky can clear

White gray to blue by the time I reach the silt

At the bottom of the glass

Or what we call blue

In time for the legislated stroll

In time for the garden party

Or what we call a garden

I want this to be a symbol

So I say it is a symbol

A swift upturning

Where the concussive browbeat

Of the compulsive order

Is flipped like a rack of ribs

Onto tender baby skin

As if desire were will

As if our hands were new

We are out of milk for coffee

Our options are

Go to the store, get pregnant, milk the bottle brush tree

We do neither we do none

Our success is five bottles between the four of us

Our success is friendship, forgiveness, non-monetary
abundance

To play the game, you put the chips in your mouth and
swish them about

It's a kind of chalky plastic

I can see behind your right eye

ABBA returns to life they never left

I wouldn't call it going to bed so much as a six hour bow

Our success is waking up

The needle in its groove

The gazelle's elongated ear

And now it's time to check on the seeds

I am impatient

When it comes to seeds

Patient when it comes to "my career"

I'd prefer the lam

They call this a nightshade?

The sun is shining so the vines are climbing

The tops of the starts have been munched

Some creature is feasting

They call it a cost-of-living raise

Maybe now I can afford to enroll in survival school

Rub two sticks together

Dowse water

Become stretchy

The commons are all around us?

I go to the mall?

They call it Shellmound

Dig a hole, toll the bones

Enumerate the dead

Mark the field branch in common

As the burrowers know

As the blue sky gray sky blue

Someone on this block is breathing

As if they cannot breathe

Some man is yelling, slamming something

A large metal box with a brick?

I am in the spindly chair

Listening from behind a fence

Thinking hearing

Thinking men

I dropped my paws into the cold spring

And was afraid

And never left California

And did not call myself fit

I like throwing balls and catching them

Their stretchy mesh says WORLD PEACE

Their worn cotton says HEC DOLLAZ

The chunk lodged in my head

The bready part of the dream

Should I open my ears?

Should I take this pillow off my knocker?

It will rain Thursday

I will go to work

You said please take care

I was afraid

I do not love it

Let this life be more than

An apparatus for producing an ever-greater quantity

Of feelings, of shoes

Dipping the stick, marking the rise

Quick everyone learn to swim

Because some of it is trapped in the atmosphere as heat

Because we can't afford to live

And it's only Tuesday

One way to relieve sunstroke

Is to cover your friend in ice

The earth does not want us

The demand from which I come

The demand with which I can't comply

The damage cost of emitting each breath

The economy requires, the economy requires

Well what does life require

Another day trading waste

I stick the branch in the ground like you told me

I did it I did it

I placed the root in the ground

I don't want to live

As if living were a way of acquiring things

Never let it be said that sitting in the sun is not a pastime

Star soaked and breezing under the hill

Yellow pistil blazing but can we eat it

The bay goes on

I wake up to it buzzing west of the highway

Full and fragrant as ever

No malicious force has set a drain to it

I closed my eyes for eight straight hours

And no one drained the bay

Though being wakeful is no guarantee against drainage

Things can and do disappear all the time

Does the forest know its distance from shore?

To what force it owes its green?

Things can and do disappear all the time

This apparatus is delusional, brands "offenders"

That apparatus creates then punishes the poor

Where they sleep

Where they shit

Where they spring like rock against rock

A slice right where the finger bends

To cling to anything

To hold onto the spoon

I didn't sail the ship

Or dip the tip in hollow

But I ate the meat

And wore the shirt

Am I holding the whip?

Bare feet, fresh coffee, a roof not yet caved

Utter luxury

Count me obligated

Shall I incorporate my hatred as a directive want

Or let loose of it

To split shell on shale

To drive west when that black cloud moves east

Whose tail is that?

The earth is round

And where will the river be then

And who will swim in it

Bury me with the wood of trees

And music made of what remains

Any fire will tell you

All my things in a heap

At the bottom of the bag

I saw the death of the earth in a child's toy

I saw grasping in the thicket

My hand was there too

Splayed out in the corner booth

We split a gin drink then another

This one's for the housing market

This one's for escape plans

The suture oozes

I wobble home

Read the future through the moldy roses

The latch on the gate is broken

I push and pull and nothing comes

Hand on the curve of your back

Hand on the lip of the wind

Despite the blood red talk

I am not a nihilist

I believe despite myself

Depicted in this diagram is a baby contemplating an egg

It does not seem to me to be a human egg

But what do I

What have I ever known

Having never been inside my own body

Mutual exclusivity is an invention

She says confidently

It never occurred to me

Someone had to be the first to say it

I prefer the coextensive

I prefer languid feasts

Feting what is insightful and generous and kind

What's the line?

"You should praise me"

Who said that?

I praise the sea

This is an old machine with a pulley

It makes music work

You have three minutes to do your song

Or the wax ends

There is disagreement about the advisability of
    transmitting

Basically

Will it serve as a memorial

Or a message

And what is the difference

The world will end

Did you read that article

Basically

No food no sky no rest no breath

No going outside

Cracking open the country to get at the yolk

Calling it finance, calling it the market requires

Yanking all the edibles away

Like a magician with their table cloth

You can't eat a useless nest of microcredit

Sealed in a silo

You can't eat mountains of smoke and candied cancer
gems

They train the cadre to believe

Hunger is the result of laziness

Every few days they shovel it off and repitch it

The cruisers crush the flowers

To produce an object lesson

The cruisers parade the street

Crushing the flowers

Is a hole in the head needed?

A hole in the head is not needed

Inextricably bound

Pushed out

Never intended to survive

Headfast into a parallel hole

On it in it or near it

I have never seen a shirt of nettles

Nor a nettle shirt

To sting the body of a boss with

Evaporative star

Anticipatory blue

Where is my coat

Where is my outing

All this work

And no tub to bathe it off

My love asks what's a Sunset pig?

All these years I just assumed

I go on assuming

Pushing down afterthoughts

Through no mind of my own

"The stakes are myself"

I'm more than a breathing apparatus?

A job to lance me to it

The stakes are see-through

See them there?

Very little news comes out of the forest

Sometimes the stone-pelters send messages

I hop in the jeep and head for the jetty

I am with the moon

My manner of eating is rumination

I keep my ears and eyes and all other holes peeled for you

In telling this story, I emphasize excrement

Asking who really owes what to whom

The scaffolding collapses

We slurp bugs and bivalves and dirty our drinking cups
    with juices

The juices are extracted, purified, and hoarded

Not being able to pay the fee, I am taken to dry dock

My ear is nailed to a post

Its wings make a shadow on the dirt

There is division between the spheres

My manner of eating is rumination

Don't this nectarine look just like the moon?

I'm mostly unconcerned with narrative

I'm no good at weaving elongation

In a fog walking you get wet

I say woman but mean person

That person

Ascending toward the moon

Rock of the sky

Rock of the face

It is raining on green Missouri

A whistling projectile

A basket of light

The air is heavy and dewy in Kansas

As if bioluminescence were plain

As if a sunrise were

I call it tropical

But there is no ocean to see

If I meet it

Halfway

If I meet it

In ambitionless affection

Following the sunlight around the house

The egg on which I stand

Moist and loose of tongue

I do not know the limits of possibility

I do not know what is possible

"What springs move us"

"And the cause of all our different gaits"

Led by the ears like a flock to the crane

Dutiful, if not loving

The salt fish and wine

Watching the sun set on Pacific East Mall

Three bands of pastel light

Return to the water through the gills of the fish

And to the air through the lungs of air-breathing land
    animals

Missing in the models is a proxy

Of the past preserved in pollen

And the cloud subroutine

Is emotion melodic?

Will I live another 30 years

I like that horse because it is a mystery to me

And paper thin wings

Where the only choice is refusal

I walk into the sun

Glaciated and sauceless

If I didn't I might as well have

Standing on the mesa

Wondering what makes a mesa

Casting was what we decided the beach was

Those who live in watery houses shouldn't cast nets

The past is not ebullient

What I thought was clarity

A knotty burl thrown up among cables

Where I am conscripted, sullen, lazy

As best I can breathe

Walking down the street

Cheek in the gravel

Hole on my face

My life will end

My life will end

If I love you I will always love you

Tomatoes in February

Seabirds at Mono Lake

The tree collapses under weight of its own fruit

This is not a metaphor

I saw it like the ocean I saw with my own eyes

And the day the meaty tissue of the mushroom became
    real

PECK BOX

When the sun goes down

The spirits come out

We huff on a pinwheel

And say it spins of its own accord

Rolling out the bins in saturated air

Oiling the slop to ease extraction

Accumulate, hoard, die, repeat

First I thought salt was just salt

Then I got worse

First I thought dirt is dirt

Not matter out of place

Not unimproved real estate

Under the fingernails

Pooled in the pockmarks

The penal is never not pertinent

If dogs are buried like dogs

That is, not at all

And if I don't want to be eaten

It is because I don't want to be turned into shit

Live from little hill

Where the chard crib's aching for more sunlight

And this vat of beans hums

The song of reproduction

Who manicures, who mops

Who mucks up the air with guttural assumption

For every private matter

There is a failure of the collective

Hastening our transformation into money

I poke at the oranges in my felt-tipped tricorne

I push two fingers into the clammed-up root bulk

That right there is a punchable pasty

That right there is the moral arc of the universe

Trending towards dog shit

The border is built

Of insistence and repetition

The sea is a carpet under which we sweep the reeking

As fish do not live in cities

The sun does not shine in a womb

Sometimes I stow in a scarred over lobe

At a repose past persuasion

The mountain is no obstacle

If there's no notion to climb it

How many years has this bottlebrush been burning

And how many more will it continue to drop red tendrils

Across the surface of the creaking earth

I notice when light is lacking

Blossom-end rot, failure to thrive

How do you take your spritz?

Evergreen bitters, debt-inducing anti-aging scrub

I take my eye wash in the cookhouse

The crow takes its charge to the street

You come to me agape

Where palms spread their wings

I knew time to be a trap

As my blood slumbers

As my blood is not mine

One does not need a theory of navigation

To know where they take the inflamed

Some of the species

Assemble on a break in the canopy

And cultivate bulbs exclusively

One does not forbid something

Which no one wants to do or have done

I almost go so far as to say

What I then say

Your departure evicts me

From softest bed of bright dew

As post-coital sun streams through the blinds

Another state-sponsored death

What does it mean to love amid the terror?

What has it ever meant?

Meet me in the dust

Where plurality's a given grove

The firewall is porous

The claptrap a sieve

In the strained silence of the gone world

Having some uh, having some trouble with these
    swaddling blinders

I am practically swinging a pheasant

In midday optimism

The deeper into the surf you go

The calmer it is

I remember coach admonishing us to come alive

Being struck by the beauty of that command

The breadth of its potential application

Yet my face is full of slop & I can't lift it

Are you in the industry?

Fuck the self-entrepreneurial

Every cow deserves a palace

To live without predetermination

To watch the thick blue mist roll in

Bobbing up the Yuba

Breaking the will of the men

With their racist stick & pokes

Rock with the face of a face

Rock with the mouth of a dog

We load onto granite slabs

And thank the earth for reptilian repair

The mountain is no obstacle

If there's no notion to climb it

The moon in its easements

The corn fat on its stalk

Where light breaks

Where subjects meet

In confident prodigality

Feasting and saying it is fasting

Sliding in wingtips the whole way down

The slippery pole of justice

"A unity of the potentially killable"

A gendered terror of the spectrum

My thesis survives not the smallest brush with

Leaving the house

My thesis which is no thesis at all

That I live and breathe and you do too

The truth recurs

Though its vestments may be novel

More officers arrive but none attempt aid

In the woundable body the primordial call

Phoning just to breathe into the receiver

I answer because I was already answerable

Not because you look like me

I want autonomy based in relation

Affluence without abundance

Having no word for this

Because I have no concept

Rapt at the effusive crack

Lapping up the overrunneth

Where does the honey hide?

What are the habits of a creature

Thrown from safety from the first?

The neonate comes under renewed attention

The future comes of its own propulsion

Every time we step on that stone it rocks

Hold me at the radiant fork

Where clams split open

Where sprouts spring miraculously to life

Bernadette says everything must be free

It's no wonder that sing and sign are sisters

The metal in the moon

Older than that

I guess I was driven through that tree

Though I don't remember it

I guess my brother and sister were too

"For me the dead are in my body. that's where heaven is"

A swollen seed coat

Among the boughs

I come and call you a flower

Shattered body, reclaim your life

Deem the norm the terror

ACKNOWLEDGMENTS

Little Hill takes its name from the city of El Cerrito, where I live on Ohlone land (www.muwekma.org) on a street which meets the hill—before colonization, indigenous Ohlone lived along the creek at the base of this hill.

"Moveable C" takes its name from Ornette Coleman, as quoted in an obituary in the *New York Times* (6/12/15):

> When he learned to play the saxophone—at first using an alto saxophone his mother gave him when he was around 14—he had not yet understood that, because of transposition between instruments, a C in the piano's "concert key" was an A on his instrument. When he learned the truth, he said, he developed a lifelong suspicion of the rules of Western harmony and musical notation.
>
> In essence, Mr. Coleman believed that all people had their own tonal centers. . . .
>
> "I've learned that everyone has their own moveable C," he said. . . [H]e identified this as "Do," the nontempered start of anyone singing or playing a "do-re-mi" major-scale sequence.

Thank you to the editors of Push Press, The Elephants, PEN America, BOMB *Magazine*, and *Harper's Magazine* for publishing poems from this book.

Endless gratitude to my friends.